GRACE
The Jeff Buckley Story

WRITTEN BY
TIFFANIE DEBARTOLO

ART BY
PASCAL DIZIN *and* LISA REIST

First Second
New York

First Second

Published by First Second
First Second is an imprint of Roaring Brook Press,
a division of Holtzbrinck Publishing Holdings Limited Partnership
175 Fifth Avenue, New York, NY 10010

Don't miss your next favorite book from First Second!
For the latest updates go to firstsecondnewsletter.com and sign up for our enewsletter.

Library of Congress Control Number: 2018938067

Paperback ISBN: 978-1-59643-287-1
Hardcover ISBN: 978-1-250-19692-7

Our books may be purchased in bulk for promotional, educational, or business use.
Please contact your local bookseller or the Macmillan Corporate and Premium Sales Department
at (800) 221-7945 ext. 5442 or by email at MacmillanSpecialMarkets@macmillan.com.

First edition, 2019

Edited by Mark Seigel and S.I. Rosenbaum
Book design by Chris Dickey
Color by Lisa Reist

Penciled with a Wacom Cintiq and Clip Paint Studio, an Apple Pencil and Procreate on an
iPad Pro, and whatever mechanical pencil was handy. Inked with a Pigma Micron and a
Pentel Brush Pen. An Apple Pencil and various Georg Vw's Brushes with Procreate on an
iPad Pro were used to ink and color.

Printed in China

Paperback: 10 9 8 7 6 5 4 3 2 1
Hardcover: 10 9 8 7 6 5 4 3 2 1

Chapter One

4

21

Chapter Two

Get lost.

Wait! I can pull a rabbit out of here!

Ta-da!

MANAGER

SLAM!

BACK HOME AT: STANTON ST

I can't just sit around writing songs every day. I've been doing this for years. I need gigs!

I told my friend Daniel about you. He said there's a cool café over on St. Marks called Sin-é that you should check out.

I know that place! I gave the owner a tape the last time I was there.

Nice kitty, Spinach.

SWIPE!

Hi, Spinach.

Where have you been? I was worried.

I've never made made a decision this big before.

I'm scared.

Me too.

Making records, going on tour. It's everything I've always wanted. Why am I so afraid?

Because you want to protect your art.

I can sign this deal and still protect my art, right?

What's going to happen to us if you go off and tour the world?

CONTRACT

Columbia Records Exclusive Recording Agreement

This contract between **COLUMBIA RECORDS** (herein-after referred to as the "Agreement") executed and effective this ___ day of ____, 1992 by and between Jeff Buckley (hereinafter referred to as the "Artist") and Columbia Records (hereinafter referred to as the "Company");

IT IS HEREBY AGREED

Artist shall produce three LP's (Untitled LP1 the Companies option to produ

Chapter Three

BEARSVILLE STUDIOS
Woodstock, NY

Chapter Four

SOAP

What is
that?

People
THE
50

★ DIET FOR A NEW AMERICA

Chapter Five

I'm beginning to wonder if I have another record in me.

I feel like I'm losing my mind.

Gotta write more songs. Better songs. Great songs. It's been almost three years since Grace. What the fuck am I doing? Am I a hack? A has-been? A never was? A no-hit wonder?

I wasn't raised like this. My mother raised me to know myself.

Who you talking to, buddy?

You don't understand. By the time my father was my age, he'd made *nine* records already. And I'm *better* than he was.

I need to get out of here. Out of this bar and out of this city.

I PREPARED MY ENTIRE LIFE TO FACE THE FUTURE, UNPREPARED TO FACE THE FUTURE.

BUT I'M LEARNING.

I HOPE I EXPLODE FROM THE LESSONS.

Chapter Six

GASP!

BARRISTERS Presents:

EVERY MONDAY NIGHT!

JEFF BUCKLEY

?

Look!

EVERY MONDAY NIGHT!

Hold it! What day is it today?

HUG!

It's Monday! It's tonight!

Would it be all right if I go with you?

I would like that.

Can it be...like... a date?

Gulp. Yeah.

What's that?

Nothing.

BARRISTERS

Let me see it.

I'm glad we're having this talk. This is important work. It could be dangerous. I cannot fuck around.

Have we met before?

DING DING!

Hey... Don't I know you? ...Fisher King!

I... work here.

He can see that, dope.

Hey, Alice, right? You work here too?! I love this place, especially the maple glazed.

That's my favorite too! Just a sec, I'll grab you one.

I listened to your tape.

They're really rough versions, and I don't even—

It was good.

Really?

Really.

You play around town much?

No.

Why not?

Fisher King, all you need is a little help and a swift kick in the ass.

You're never gonna make it if you don't get out there and start playing live.

Let me ask you something—

Can you tune a guitar?

Yeah.

Chapter Seven

MAY 27. 1997

HONK, HONK!

This is where you live?

Isn't it great?

Keith Foti. Gene hired me to help bring down the gear.

We need to get everything over to the rehearsal space this afternoon.

May 29, 1997

Chapter Eight

151

After Jeff died, his mother developed a roll of film she found in his camera. These are candid photos he took while on tour.

Here's one of Michael.

Jeff takes a selfie in the mirror.

Another shot Jeff took while on tour. This one is of Mick.

Jeff and
the crew.

In a hotel room,
on the road.

Jeff in a hotel room, on the phone with the president of Columbia Records, Donny Lenner. Jeff had just told Lenner that they couldn't give his song "Forget Her" to Aerosmith, and if they tried to give it to anyone else, he'd go back to singing at Sin-é.

Jeff and his mother, Mary Guibert, just before he moved to New York.

Mountains of love to the First Second Books crew:
Mark Siegel, Sara Rosenbaum, Robyn Chapman, Andrew Arnold, and
Gina Gagliano. Oceans of gratitude to Pascal Dizin, Lisa Reist, and
Tiffanie DeBartolo for their artistry, their craft, and their grace. Supreme
adoration and profound humility for the love and support of my accomplices
in life and my dearest friends, Alison Raykovich and Conrad Rippy.
And, last but most certainly not least, thanks to Jeff's fans,
who remember him and keep his songs wafting on the winds.

—Mary Guibert

I would like to give much love and thanks to:

Mary Guibert, Gene Bowen, Jack Bookbinder, Mark Siegel,
Pascal Dizin, and Lisa Reist.

My family: Candy DeBartolo, Eddie DeBartolo, Lisa DeBartolo,
Nikki DeBartolo, Asher, Milo, Jasper, Don, and Chad.

My husband and hero, Scott Schumaker.

And finally to Jeff Buckley, with love, grace, and gratitude forever.

—Tiffanie DeBartolo